THE ESSENTIAL AUTOMOBILE

Published by WordCrafts Press
Cody, Wyoming 82414
www.wordcrafts.net

THE ESSENTIAL AUTOMOBILE

Ralph E. Jarrells

WordCrafts

Contents

The Beginning of the Car 1

Relevant History...
  The Amazing Chronological History of the Car 5

Leonardo da Vinci
  Father of the Car? 15

Dumb & Funny Car Stuff 17

Did you know?
  The Car—a Solution to Pollution 30

Mine's Bigger Than Yours! Mine's Faster Than Yours!
  The Beginning of Automobile Racing 36

21st Century Philosophers
  The License Plate Writers 46

Road Side Attractions & Highway Advertising 67

First Came the Car—Part 2 79

Epilogue 86

Chapter 1

THE BEGINNING OF THE CAR

Much of the early history of the automobile is funny by today's standards. Those early cars looked more like the horse drawn carriages of their day.

Others, like the Oruktor Amphobolos, resembled a steam powered paddle wheel boat.

Fig. 47.—Evans's "Oruktor Amphibolis," 1804.

Many people are surprised to find out that the first recorded reference to the automobile is found in the Bible.

> *"The chariots storm through the streets,*
> *rushing back and forth through the squares.*
> *They look like flaming torches;*
> *they dart about like lightning."*
> Nahum 2:4

There is a strong case to be made that the fathers of the modern automobile were English Franciscan philosopher, Roger Bacon (c1220-1292) and Italian Renaissance man, Leonardo da Vinci. It was Bacon's c1270 prediction,

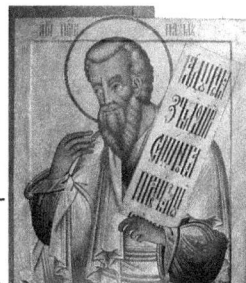

"chariots will travel with incredible speed without the aid of any animal." This prematurely accurate resulted in Bacon being thrown in jail for *"being in league with the devil."*

Da Vinci, on the other actually provided the drawings of a self-propelled vehicle. His spring-propelled vehicle signed in c1478 has been produced and proven to work.

For the earliest experiments in automotive history, we have to travel to the English countryside. It was Christmas Eve, 1801. The farmers in a local area of Cornwall were alarmed by a loud noise, shattering the quiet of their countryside. Many ran out of their homes to see Richard Trevithick piloting his new invention—a steam driven, horse-less carriage. It was noisy with its huge metal and wooden wheels and filled the area with excessive amounts of wood smoke. But it would carry passengers and travel at nearly 10 miles per hour. It was an important date looking back but neither Trevithick nor his neighbors were overly impressed with "his toy." He actually disassembled the "first automobile" and sold the engine to a local mill owner.

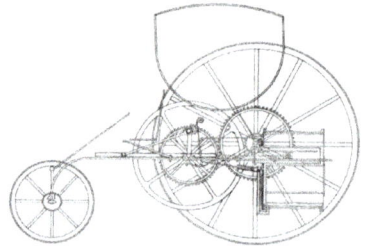

Thanks, in part, to Trevithick's success and other inventor-developers, England and the European continent took the lead in the development and manufacturing of automobiles. But, these early, mostly steam-driven vehicles ran into strong opposition from stagecoach and railroad operators who were joined by farmers and turnpike owners. As a result of this strong lobby, the British Parliament passed a number of laws restricting the use of automobiles, the strongest of which was the Red Flag Act. Adopted

in 1865, it required a person to walk ahead of all "road locomotives" (as the Brits call these early automobiles) to warn others of the approaching vehicle. The Red Flag Act which was in effect until 1896 and all but destroyed England's opportunity to continue to lead in automobile development. This opened the door for France, Germany and the United States.

Trevithick inspires a Cornish doctor, Goldsworthy Gurney to design his own steam-powered carriage. A successful design that carried as many as 6 passengers made the trip for London to Bath in 1829. The average 15 MPH, including stops, showed the ability to offer commercial service. Gurney made a number of design improvements in his machines increasing their reliability and distance. His commercial passenger business failed due to high taxes said to be pushed by the horse-drawn coach industry.

The automotive industry in the U.S. was moving ahead as well. In 1789, Oliver Evan of Philadelphia received a U.S. Patent for his "Steam Land Carriage." He was successful in developing a steam-driven river dredge in 1804 and his river dredge was the basic design for his steam-driven vehicle that he called the Orukor Amphobolos. His 15.5 ton design combined his steam-driven dredge, a flatboat attached to a heavy wagon and a series of belts and gears that transmitted power to the wagon wheels. His invention started as a river dredge but, the need to get the dredge from Evan's workshop the one and a half miles to the river resulted in the first self-propelled vehicle in America. Evan's design never caught on and neither did his vehicle name, but his prophetic pronouncement did, "the time will come when people will travel in stages moved by steam engines, from one city to another, almost as fast as birds can fly."

The next major development in automobiles in the U.S. was driven

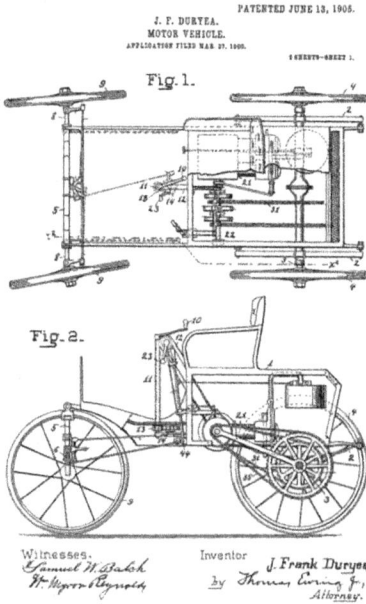

PATENTED JUNE 13, 1905.
J. F. DURYEA.
MOTOR VEHICLE.
APPLICATION FILED MAR. 27, 1900.

Fig. 1.

Fig. 2.

Witnesses.
Inventor J. Frank Duryea
by Thomas Living Jr,
Attorney.

by Charles and Frank Duryea. The bicycle manufacturing brothers combined their knowledge of bicycle design with their interest in developing a motor car. Earlier designs were generally modifications of horse drawn carriages to accommodate some kind of motor. The Duryeas started from scratch. The success with their first design in 1893 and their second in 1895 led them to apply for a patent on March 27, 1900 and become the first company founded in the U.S. for the purpose of making automobiles. Their patent was granted June 13,1905.

Henry Ford is credited with creating the modern assembly line for manufacturing in 1914. Prior to the innovation each car was individually hand made. Before the assembly line it took 12 hours to assemble a Model T. With the assembly line, a new Model T rolled off the conveyor belt every 24 seconds. This increased manufacturing efficiency to the point where the price of the first Model T was $850 in 1908. In 1915 the price had dropped to $440.00 and to $290.00 in 1925. So, it was Henry Ford who brought automobile ownership to almost everyone in the U.S.

Chapter 2

RELEVANT HISTORY...
THE AMAZING CHRONOLOGICAL
HISTORY OF THE CAR

D uring the early years, even the naming of these vehicles seems humorous as well as the descriptive. George Selden patented the "road machine." The Duryea brothers had their "motor wagon." Henry Ford's first design was called the "Quadricycle." Other names included autometon, pleo locomotive, autokenetic, buggyaut, motor-vique, automotor horse, motorig and the horseless carriage. In 1897, the New York Times made it official "…the new mechanical wagon with the awful name—utomobile, has come to stay." The article went on to say, "sooner or later they will displace the fashionable carriage of the present hour. Sensitive and emotional folk cannot view the impending change without conflicting emotions. Man loves the horse and he is not likely to love the automobile. Nor will he ever get used to speeding along the road behind nothing."

615BC – Prophet Nahum predicted:

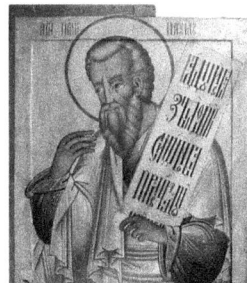

"The chariots storm through the streets, rushing back and forth through the squares. They look like flaming torches;they dart about like lightning."

Nahum 2:4

1270 – Roger Bacon English philosopher predicts the creation of "chariots that would travel with incredible speed without the aid of any animal."

c1478 – Leonardo da Vinci produces sketches of the self-moving car (Chapter 3).

1548 – Nostradamus, known for many accurate predictions, said in 1548, "from Albion's shore shall come a marvelous conveyance, a carriage silincieus bearing the arms of Rolles De Roi." (Rolls Royce?)

1680 – Dutch physicist, Christian Huygens, designed the first internal combustion engine that was to run on gunpowder. Thankfully, it was never built.

1690 – Denis Papin made the first public proposal of a piston driven vehicle. Papin was noted as the inventor of the pressure cooker.

1769 – The first recorded success of a self-powered vehicle was by a French military engineer, Nicolas Joseph Cugnot. The three wheeled, steam-powered vehicle was built to move large artillery pieces. It was slow (2 to 3 mph) and extremely awkward to maneuver, however, it was successful in moving by its own power. Some accounts have this event in 1770, others in 1768.

1769 – The first automobile accident occurred and Cugnot's test was short lived. He crashed into a wall severely damaging the vehicle and the wall.

1789 - Oliver Evans is granted the first U.S. patent for an automobile that he calls a "steam land carriage."

1791 – On December 17, the city of New York passes a traffic regulation that creates the first streets that allow traffic in only one direction or "One Way."

1792 – First toll roads opened in U.S., which were in Pennsylvania and Connecticut, for cars and carriages.

1794 – John Staples is granted a patent on April 25th for the construction of "a carriage to be propelled by mechanical powers." The perpetual motion vehicle was never built.

1801 – The first internal combustion engine vehicle was built in Cornwall England by Richard Trevithick. Four days after his successful test run the new vehicle went up in flames.

1804 – Oliver Evans demonstrated his "steam land carriage" that he called an Orukor Amphibolos Latin for amphibious dredge.

1807 – Francois Isaac de Rivaz of Switzerland invented an internal combustion engine that used a mixture of hydrogen and oxygen as fuel. This design proved to be totally unsuccessful. It was an idea that is currently being revisited.

1860 – Etienne Lenoir built and patented the first commercially successful gasoline engine in France.

1865 – Red Flag Act becomes law in England taking English inventors out of the automobile race.

1867 – The first "getaway" is recorded. A cop, on foot, is left behind by an 1867 model steam-powered car.

1867 – The first roadside billboards are leased.

1867 – Eugene Langen and Nikolas August Otto introduced a four-stroke Otto engine in Deuts, Germany. Gottlieb Daimler (who would be better known in the future for his relationship with Carl Benz) was involved in the design.

1868 – The first traffic light (gas) went into service in Parliament Square, London, on December 10. It was invented by J. P. Knight.

1869 – On January 2, just 23 days after its initial installation, the first gas traffic light exploded injuring a constable.

1885 – Carl Benz successfully tested his first gasoline engine automobile in Mannheim, Germany. In another part of Germany, that same year, Gottlieb Daimler successfully tested his all-purpose engine.

1888 – On July 27, the first electric car, a tricycle run by a battery was designed by Boston inventor, Phillip Pratt.

1893 – Henry Ford completed his first car in a Detroit garage at 2am, June 4th.

1893 - Brothers Charles and J. Frank Duryea introduced and successfully operated what is generally considered the first successful internal combustion powered horseless carriage in the U.S. on September 21st.

1895 – The Duryea brothers' 1-cylinder, 4-stroke automobile

won the first American road race, Chicago to Evanston, in the middle of a blizzard. The other competitor, in a Benz, gave up after developing a sever case of frostbite.

1895 – The Duryea Motor Wagon Company, established by the Duryea brothers, made the first commercially available gasoline cars.

1896 – George H. Morill, Jr., of Massachusetts, was the first purchaser of a gasoline powered car.

1896 – Charles B. King drove his horseless carriage on the streets of Detroit and became the first person to drive a car in "Motor City" on March 6th.

1896 – The first automobile accident occurred on May 30th in New York City when a Duryea driven by Henry Wells of Springfield, MA collided with a bicycle ridden by Evylyn Thomas of New York.

1896-The first death attributed to an automobile was August 17, 1896 in London. Bridget Driscoll, age 45, was killed crossing the Crystal Palace grounds The coroner concluded that the car was traveling 4mph and added his hope there would be no further deaths due to driving.

1897 – George Smith became the first person arrested for drunken driving on September 10th.

1898 – Travelers Insurance issued the first automobile insurance policy to Dr. Truman Martin, Buffalo, NY.

1898 – Duryea Auto, Peoria, IL, produced the

first "armored car." It sported a Colt machine gun.

1898 – New York City Police officers used bicycles to pursue speeding motorists.

1899 – Newport, RI became the location of the first motor parade. 19 of the young women from the area plastered their family motor cars with wisteria, strutting their stuff in single file.

1899 – Jacob German, a New York City cab driver, was nabbed for speeding. Mr. German was driving 12 mph. He was booked and jailed.

1899 – The first automotive death in the U.S. is Henry Bliss in New York on September 13, 1899.

1901 – Oldsmobile becomes the first mass-produced automobile manufacturing 425 vehicles in that year.

1901 – New York became the first state to require owners to register their cars, April 25th. That year 954 car owners paid $1 to display 3" high, custom-made initial plates.

1903 – Dr. Horatio Jackson made the first cross-country car trip from San Francisco to New York City. The trip began June 18th and ended 3 months later on August 1st.

1903 – Police set up the first organized speed traps.

1903 – Massachusetts became the first state to begin manufacturing license plates. They were porcelain-enameled plates—white on blue.

1903 – Bathtub maker David Dunbar Buick started the Buick Motor Car company in Flint, MI.

1904 – Mr. Rolls met Mr. Royce.

1905 – The first car was reported stolen in St. Louis.

1907 – The first President of the United States to ride in a car was Theodore Roosevelt in Lansing, MI. The Oldsmobile was driven by Ransom E. Olds.

FATALLY HURT BY AUTOMOBILE.

Vehicle Carrying the Son of ex-Mayor Edson Ran Over H. H. Bliss, Who Was Alighting from a Trolley Car.

H. H. Bliss, a real estate dealer, with offices at 41 Wall Street, and living at 235 West Seventy-fifth Street, was run over last night at Central Park West and Seventy-fourth Street. He was injured fatally.

Bliss, accompanied by a woman named Lee, was alighting from a south-bound Eighth Avenue trolley car, when he was knocked down and run over by an automobile in charge of Arthur Smith of 151 West Sixty-second Street. He had left the car, and had turned to assist Miss Lee, when the automobile struck him. Bliss was knocked to the pavement, and two wheels of the cab passed over his head and body. His skull and chest were crushed.

Dr. David Orr Edson, son of ex-Mayor Edson, of 38 West Seventy-first Street, was the occupant of the electric cab. As soon as the vehicle was brought to a standstill he sent in a call to Roosevelt Hospital for an ambulance, and until its arrival did all he could to aid the injured man. When he was taken to the hospital Dr. Marny, the house surgeon, said that Bliss was so seriously injured that he could not live.

Smith was arrested and locked up in the West Sixty-eighth Street Station. It is claimed that a large truck occupied the right side of the avenue, making it necessary for Smith to run his vehicle close to the car. Dr. Edson was returning from a sick call in Harlem when the accident happened.

Mr. Bliss boarded at 233 West Seventy-fifth Street. The place where the accident happened is known to the motormen on the trolley line as "Dangerous Stretch," on account of the many accidents which have occurred there during the past Summer.

1907 – The first taxi cabs made it to the streets in New York City on August 13th.

1908 - General Motors Company was founded by William Crapo Dyrant.

1908 – Rhode Island became the first state to require state drivers licenses.

1908 – On October 1st the first Model T Ford was revealed.

1909- - The first rural mile of concrete pavement in the U.S. was opened in Wayne County MI.

1911 – The first lines designating traffic lanes were painted, in white, on River Road near Trenton MI. Motorists, intrigued by the lines, did their best to straddle them. It's a practice still observed by many today.

1913 – Gulf Refining Company became the first company to sell gallons of gas from a drive-in station. The "pump station" was located in Pittsburgh and it stayed open all night. The claim was disputed by the Central Oil Company who claimed their 1910 station built in Detroit was the first.

1913-Gulf was the first company to distribute free road maps in this year.

1913 – On September 10th, the first paved coast-to-coast highway opened.

1914 – The first stop sign were installed in Detroit. They were manually operated stop and go signs.

1914 – The first electric lighted traffic signals were installed in Cleveland, OH. Not knowing what they were for, many accidents resulted due to motorists gawking at the newly erected, red and green lights,

1915 – The first ever-recorded rebate for buying a car was instituted by Ford. Each purchaser got a $50 rebate

because Ford surpassed its sales goal for that year.

1916 – President Woodrow Wilson signed the Federal Aid Road Act establishing the first national highway system.

1916 – 55% of all of the cars in the world were FORD Model T's, a record that has never been beaten.

1918 – The first three colored traffic lights were installed in Detroit, MI.

1919 – Oregon became the first state to enact a gasoline tax. The $.01 per gallon tax was to be used for road construction.

1923 – The first Checker cab was completed June 18, 1923.

1924 – Statistics were released that showed one in every seven people in the U.S. owned an automobile.

1929 – 26 million cars were registered in the U.S.

1933 – The first drive-in theater was built opening on June 6th in Camden, NJ. The feature? *Wife Beware* staring Adolphe Menjou. (See Chapter 8)

1933 – The first Soap Box Derby was held August 18-19 in Dayton, OH. Randall Custer was the winner.

1935 – The first parking meter was erected on July 16th in Oklahoma City. Five cents bought 60 minutes. The

inventor, Carl C. Magee, was granted patent #2,118,318 issued May 24, 1938,

1937 – The first automobile/airplane was manufactured. The "Arrowbile" cruises at 105 mph, has a top flight speed of 120 mph and comes with a 6-cylinder Studebaker engine was the invention of Waldo Waterman. It's the first of many strangely wonderful inventions from, where else, California.

1948 – Harley Earl introduced the "tail fin" on the Cadillac.

1953 – The first curbside mike is introduced, adding greatly to the efficiency of the drive-in restaurant.

1976 – Pointe Coupee Funeral Home, New Roads, Los Angeles, CA, installed the first drive-by picture window to make visiting the dearly departed more convenient.

Chapter 3

LEONARDO DA VINCI
FATHER OF THE CAR?

The genius behind two of the World's most famous and contro-versial paintings, The Last Supper and the Mona Lisa, is the designer of a self-propelled vehicle that could easily have been the forerunner of the modern automobile. As a designer, Leonardo da Vinci is not as well known as a painter but his genius shines with equal magnitude. The Atlantic Codex, a portfolio of design drawings by da Vinci included initial concepts for the airplane, the helicopter, the submarine, the tank, the parachute, the steam engine and many other devices we use today. And, on sheet 812r, penned in 1478 when Leonardo was 24 years old, is the design. sketch of the "self-propelled vehicle." It is also the first record of the word automobile.

Da Vinci's designs and three models of the "self-propelled" car have been on display in the

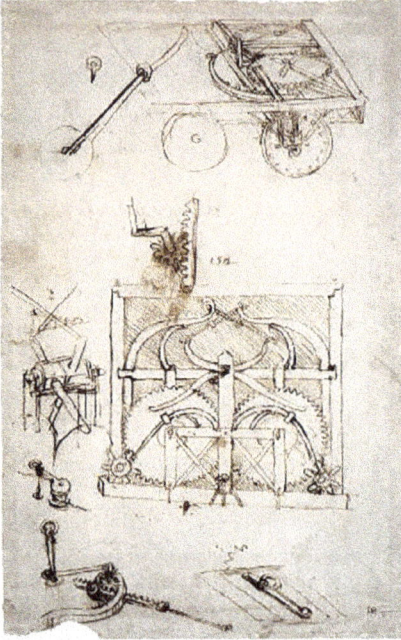

Museum of History and Science in Florence, Italy. It took 21st century computer modeling and robotics experts to create a working model of this 15th century design. A replica is also on display in the Toyota Museum in Japan.

The vehicle, sometimes called the "clockworks car" because it is propelled by springs similar to the system that runs a clock, has three wheels, is 5' by 5'6", has programmable steering and will travel about 40 meters or a little over 131 feet before the springs have to be reset. Much like a child's spring-propelled toy da Vinci's vehicle was powered by rotating the wheels in the opposite direction.

A little less than 20 years later, da Vinci's design of ball bearings is certainly the beginning of the concept vital for today's automobile. Ball bearings are found in many of the sub systems.

Chapter 4

DUMB & FUNNY CAR STUFF

E ach year The Darwin Awards are given, with tongue in cheek, honoring those humans that kill themselves in the most stupid ways. The award honors the survival of the fittest or smartest.

We start with some of the people who didn't get the award but they were in there trying hard.

James Burns, 34, of Alamo, MI, was killed as he was trying to repair what Police describe as a "farm-type truck." Burns got a friend to drive the truck on the highway while Burns hung underneath so that he could ascertain the source of a troubling noise. Burns' clothes caught on something, however, and the driver found what was left of Burns wrapped around the truck's drive shaft.

∽

A 24-year-old salesman from Hialeah, FL, was killed when his car smashed into a pole in the median strip on I95. Police said that the man was traveling 80mph and, judging by the sales manual that was found open and clutched to his chest, he had been busily reading when the accident occurred.

Firefighters summoned to a Woodinville home arrived to find twenty-foot flames shooting out of two Chevy Astro vans. After quelling the gasoline-fed blaze with water, dry chemicals, and foam, they questioned the man responsible for the incident. Turns out that our Honorable Mention winner decided to siphon gasoline with an electric wet'n'dry shop vac. Amazingly, he had managed to collect and transfer an entire bucketful of gasoline before an electrical spark ignited the fumes.

∽

And, the Darwin Award winner for 2004 is... may I have the envelope please?

The Arizona Highway Patrol discovered a pile of smoldering metal embedded in the side of a cliff rising above the road at the crest of a curve. The wreckage resembled what you would expect to find at the site of an airplane crash. But, it was a car—unidentifiable at the scene.

It took a lab to piece together the story. The driver of a 1967 Chevy Impala had purloined a JATO (Jet Assisted Take Off unit —actually a solid fuel rocket) that is used to give heavy military transport planes a "little" extra push when taking off on short airfields. The

driver found a long, straight road in the desert outside Las Vegas, attached the JATO unit to his car, jumped in, got up some speed and fired up the jet device.

By measurements made at the scene, officers calculate that the driver ignited the JATO unit about 3 miles from the crash scene. That's where the asphalt was scorched and melted.

The unit reached maximum thrust within 5 seconds, causing the Chevy to reach speeds well in excess of 350mph within 5 seconds and continuing at full power for 20 to 25 seconds until the JATO unit burned out. The driver, now pilot, was basically along for the ride since he had no means to steer of control the car.

The Chevy remained on the highway for about 2.5 miles (15 to 20 seconds) before the driver decided to applied the brakes. The result was interesting. The brakes completely melted, all four tires blew out and heavy rubber marks were left on the highway surface just a little over 1.4 miles from the crash scene. With no tires, the Chevy became airborne. Apparently the Chevy was still accelerating when it hit the cliff at a height over the highway of some 125 feet. The remains found at the bottom of a three-foot deep crater, were limited to a few small fragments of bone, teeth and hair and some fingernail shards were removed from a piece of debris believed to be a portion of the steering wheel.

Dumb Crooks and Cars

> *(Dumb Crook News is a regular feature of the John Boy & Billy Big Show. A number of the items that follow are from their archive.)*

A Police officer had found the perfect place to set a speed trap for unsuspecting speeders. But, one day, everyone that past his radar unit was under the speed limit. This was a first. The officer decided to investigate and quickly found the problem. A 10-year-old boy was standing on the side of the road some distance from the officer's trap with a huge hand painted sign that said, "Radar Trap Ahead." The officer continued his investigation and found that the 10-year-old had an accomplice. Another boy was situated about 100 yards past the trap with another sign, "TIPS." His bucket was full of change.

Authorities are calling him "The Mad Crapper." Police say the man caused over 13 thousand dollars worth of damage to six vehicles by breaking into them and defecating on their seats. Court records say he showed a definite preference for Ford Mustangs: they were his car of choice in four of the incidents. A Ford truck and an Oldsmobile Cutlass were his other two targets. Authorities say the man would scale the fence around the lot, break into cars that customers had left for repairs, and...do his thing. He is now under psychiatric care and is taking medication to control his impulses.

In a poorly judged attempt to convince his wife he was sober enough to drive, a 29-year-old husband pulled up to a State Police barracks in his pickup truck, parked illegally, and demanded a sobriety check. He failed the Breathalyzer test and was taken into custody. "Basically," an amused Sergeant Paul Slevinski explained, "his wife won the argument."

～

45 year old Amy Brasher was arrested in San Antonio after a mechanic reported to police that 18 packages of marijuana were packed in the engine compartment of the car which she had brought to the mechanic for an oil change. According to police, Brasher later said that she didn't realize that the mechanic would have to raise the hood to change the oil.

～

Members of a Norfolk family were lucky to escape with their skins intact when 90 gallons of gasoline stored in their garage unexpectedly ignited. What led to the explosion? It turns out that these candidates for Least Intelligent Life Form of the Universe had decided to stockpile gas in readiness for potential fuel blockades. They purchased large water storage cans and began collecting fuel. But the seals on water cans are not suitable for corrosive materials. The cans leaked, and flammable fumes filled the family garage—which also contained the house's central heating boiler. When the temperature in the house dropped, the boiler switched on, igniting the fumes and creating a fireball big enough to satisfy a Hollywood director.

∾

Two men who were paid to help stash some of the loot from the infamous Loomis-Fargo armored car heist got prison terms in a Charlotte, North Carolina courtroom recently. One of the men contributed yet another humorous twist to the case—spectators and court officials broke into laughter when the man's attorney admitted that his client reported his share of the loot as income on his federal tax return.

∾

In June 1992, police recovered a stolen 1980 Jaguar in mint condition—with 82 miles on the odometer—in the back yard of a man in Fairfax Station, Virginia. The car had been reported stolen from a Chevrolet dealer in Arlington on July 1, 1980, and apparently had not been driven at all since then.

∾

Newport, Delaware police didn't have any trouble tracking down a suspect wanted for leaving the scene of a traffic accident. The impact of the crash ruptured several paint cans in the bed of the suspect's pickup, leaving a trail of paint four miles long that led right into the parking lot of the his apartment complex.

∾

A Greensboro, NC police officer leaving work one evening noticed an interior light on in a car parked near the police department. Upon investigating, he discovered a drunk who had broken into the car, grabbed a handful of change from the ashtray, and passed out in the front seat. Bad choice: the vehicle was an unmarked Greensboro patrol car. The officer said the hapless thief was unconscious with the change in his hand and his head resting on the police band radio.

~

A well-endowed Kansas woman -- who was also quite intoxicated -- decided to lift her shirt and expose her "charms" to a passing train. Unfortunately, the flirty flasher got a little too close, and was sucked into the side of the train by the wind. She ended up with two broken arms and some facial lacerations, and was later charged with criminal trespassing.

~

An Arlington, Texas man pulled a gun on a couple of armored car drivers and made off with several bags of cash. The gunman didn't get far, though: he had parked his getaway car next to a bus full of Japanese tourists. Fascinated by the robbery, the tourists snapped numerous pictures of the crook and his car, including several clear shots of the car's license plate.

~

Two thieves who broke into a house in Oklahoma were caught red-handed by the resident of the home -- an Oklahoma state trooper. These were apparently not the most observant burglars in the history of crime: they had walked through the trooper's garage -- right past his marked patrol car -- on the way into the house.

~

A District Court judge in a DWI case in Winston-Salem, North Carolina asked the arresting officer to describe his probable cause for stopping the suspect's car. the officer replied: "Well, judge, he had apparently been riding for a long time with one foot on the gas, and one foot on the brakes. When he went by us, both of his front tires were on fire. We thought it might be a good idea to stop him."

Asked to describe the defendant's condition, the officer replied "He was pretty well lit -- just like the tires."

～

A suspected drug dealer was arrested after selling some crack cocaine to three Vancouver police officers, even though all three were wearing full police uniforms. The cops spotted the suspicious-looking man during a routine patrol and waved a ten-dollar bill at him. The suspect took the money and handed a small quantity of crack over to them, and was arrested immediately. He told the cops that he had noticed the uniforms, but because they were in an unmarked car, he thought they were on their way to a costume party.

～

After being shot by a pawn shop owner he had tried to rob, a would-be holdup man from Huntsville, Alabama staggered off down the street, forgetting all about his getaway car parked at the curb. Investigators later searched the vehicle and found a "to do" list that included the item, "Rob pawn shop."

～

A pair of carjackers approached a woman waiting in line at a gas station in Rome, Italy, forced her out of her car, and sped away in it. Italian police caught up with the thieves a short distance later, just after the car they had stolen from the gas station...ran out of gas.

～

LA Police spotted a man driving erratically on Hollywood street at 2 AM, and pursued him for several blocks. Wanting to dispose of the evidence, the drunken suspect opened his car door to dispose of a can of beer. Unfortunately, he wasn't wearing a seatbelt, and managed to toss himself out of the car along with the beer can. He was treated for cuts and bruises, then booked on a DUI charge.

❧

A teenager in Berlin, Germany on his way to a court hearing to face charges of leaving the scene of an accident, ran a red light. When German police stopped the teen, they discovered he was driving to his court date in...a stolen bus. Said one official: "well, at least he was on time for court."

❧

A 50-year-old Albuquerque, New Mexico man was arrested after he tried to steal three different utility trailers from a Home Depot store in a single evening. The first trailer came loose from the man's pickup and crashed a few miles from the store. The man returned and stole a second trailer, which he lost not far from the first. A sheriff's deputy happened by the second trailer and stopped to investigate, just as the man came by with a third stolen trailer hooked to his truck. The fender of the trailer clipped the deputy's car, and a slow-speed chase ensued. The deputy says the man was travelling at a leisurely 25 miles per hour, "probably because he'd learned that trailers don't stay on too well at high speeds." The hapless crook was charged with three counts of theft, along with three counts of leaving the scene of an accident.

❧

A motorist in Tulsa, Oklahoma ran a red light in full view of a police officer. When the cop turned on his blue light, the driver decided to make a run for it, leading the officer on a chase that stretched several miles and reached speeds of 100 miles per hour. The getaway came to an end at a highway tollbooth. Instead of driving around the booth or running straight through, the fugitive pulled up and stopped at the "exact change only" lane. He was still fumbling for correct change when the officer arrived to arrest him.

❧

Several men in Toronto, Canada stole a bulldozer and drove it to a local bank, where they tried to use it to rip an automated teller machine off the front of the building. The suspects almost completely destroyed the front of the bank in the attack. The only thing undamaged was...the ATM machine. The men abandoned the bulldozer in the bank's parking lot and walked away without getting any money.

∾

The Channel 13 news van was stopped at a red light on the streets of Bartow, Florida recently, when a group of loud malcontents pulled alongside and started yelling "Hey -- put us on TV!" An officer in an unmarked police cruiser happened to pull up behind the two vehicles, noticed the ruckus, and decided to run the license plate number of the second car. He quickly discovered the tag had been reported stolen. Quicker than you can say, "I wanna be a TV star," the loudmouths were completely surrounded by cops. The driver was charged with possession of the stolen tag, and his passengers were arrested on a variety of outstanding warrants. One positive note —they did get to be on Channel 13 News.

∾

A Los Angeles street gang member was killed during an attempted drive-by shooting. Police say the man was leaning out the window preparing to fire when the driver of the car he was riding in got too close to a parked car along the curb. His head collided with the rear window of the parked car.

∾

A Tampa, Florida man test-driving a new Porsche was stopped and ticketed for driving 60 in a 35-mile per-hour zone. When the man returned to the dealership, he waited for the salesman to get out of the car, then sped away. It wasn't hard for police to track the man down, since he'd just given his address to the cop who wrote him the speeding ticket. The suspect was arrested and the car was recovered at the man's home. His explanation: "I didn't steal the car —I just wanted to make sure it would fit in my garage."

～

Five men in matching bandanas robbed a McDonalds in Detroit, Michigan recently. During their escape, one gang member pulled the bandana off his head and threw it out the window of the getaway car. Unfortunately for him, the bandana got caught on the car's radio antenna, making a nice flag that attracted the attention of Detroit police, who made a quick arrest.

～

A Pennsylvania woman lost her lawsuit against the state Department of Transportation for alleged back injuries she suffered when her car skidded out of control on an icy spot in the road. The case was torpedoed by a videotape supplied by the woman's estranged husband. The tape shows the woman a year after her accident, wrestling with another bikini-clad woman in a vat of coleslaw during Bike Week in Daytona Beach, Florida.

～

A Pamela, New York motorist who was more than a little stoned and weaving from lane to lane looked up to find a police car in his rearview mirror. Seized with a major case of paranoia, the man pulled into the driveway of the first house he came to, pretending to be arriving home. His ploy might have worked, except this particular driveway belonged to the home of the very officer who was following him. The suspect was charged with DUI and possession of marijuana.

～

Seattle, Washington police sent out an A.P.B. when an 18-year-old man stole a marked police cruiser and went for a joyride. A short time later, a local patrolman radioed headquarters that he'd spotted the stolen car. An officer in the area heard the call and responded.

As Officer #1 sat at a stoplight, a second officer arrived. Officer #2, thinking he'd just spotted the stolen patrol car, rammed Officer #1. Officer #1, thinking he'd been attacked by the stolen cruiser, opened fire on Officer #2. The two cops exchanged more than 20 shots before they realized their mistake. Meanwhile, the man who'd stolen the police car got cold feet, returned to the police department, and gave himself up.

~

An Oklahoma City man who'd just been released on bail was a little too eager to head back home. The just-released crook lost his cool when a slow-moving van held him up on the highway, so he veered in front of the van and made obscene gestures at the occupants. When the van pulled into a parking lot, the angry ex-con stopped, ran over to the van, and continued his tirade. He realized his mistake when the van's seven passengers climbed out -- and turned out to be members of the Oklahoma City police department's tactical unit, all in full riot gear. As if he wasn't in enough trouble already, a check of the man's car turned up a small quantity of crack cocaine, which earned him a quick trip back to jail.

~

A motorist was unknowingly caught speeding by one of those automated photographic speed traps. He received a ticket/summons for $40 in the mail with a photo of his car with the speed, time, date and location neatly imprinted on the photo. In an effort to show his sense of humor, he sent the police department a photograph of $40. Not to be outdone, a few days later, he received a letter from the police department that contained a photograph of a pair of handcuffs.

~

As gas prices have continued to climb, siphoning gas has become an increasing problem. Siphoning is accomplished by inserting one end of a hose and sucking on the other end creating a vacuum that starts the flow of gasoline into a container. There is an art to the amount of suction and how quickly you remove the hose from your lips. A would be gas siphoner in Seattle, WA, got a lot more than he bargained for as he tried to purloin some gas from a motor home. When Police arrived the perpetrator was curled up next to the motor home. A Police spokesman said that while attempting to steal gasoline from the motor home he placed the hose into the motor home's sewage tank by mistake and hadn't totally perfected the art of siphoning.

~

A woman reported her car stolen and mentioned that her car phone was in it. The policeman taking the report called the phone. Surprisingly, the thief answered the phone. The policeman told him that he had read the car for sale ad in the newspaper and was interested in buying the car. They arranged to meet and the thief was arrested.

~

R. C. Gaitlin, 21, walked up to two police officers who were showing their squad car's computer equipment to a group of children in a Detroit neighborhood. He asked the officers how the equipment worked. When asked for a piece of identification, Gaitlin gave them his driver's license. The officers input the Gaitlin's information into their computed and promptly arrested Gaitlin. The computer provided the officers with the information that Gaitlin was wanted for a two-year-old armed robbery in St. Louis.

~

After a short chase, a Redondo Beach, CA, officer charged the driver of a white Mazda with DUI. The car had been driving down the Pacific Coast Highway with the upper half of a traffic light pole lying across the hood. When asked about the pole, the driver replied, "It came with the car when I bought it."

~

A totally wrecked Ford was found at the bottom of a 100-foot cliff in Scarborough, England. Police found no sign of the driver but they did discover a pile of human feces on the driver's seat.

~

Officers in Amhurst, NY, responded to a motor vehicle accident. They found the wrecked car with two occupants in the back seat. Later questioning revealed that the two were an intoxicated couple. Apparently, the driver of the car objected to something his wife said so he punched her in the face. She jumped in the back seat to attempt to get away from him. Not to be outdone by the move, the driver followed her into the back seat while the car was moving. The car crashed into a small clump of trees bout 15 feet off the road.

~

And, finally, a 36-year-old man called for a tow truck to get the fire truck he was driving towed out of the mud. Instead of a tow truck, California Highway Patrol arrived and locked him up. The man was drunk and the fire truck was stolen. The man said he was on a two-day drunk because of a fight with his wife. He had problems with his 1983 Chevy which he had gotten stuck in the mud. He had gone to a nearby Volunteer Fire Station to use the phone. Finding it closed, he broke in. Not finding a phone he decided to take the truck which he drove through the station's roll-up door. He got the fire truck stuck in the mud less than 20 feet from where his car was stuck in the mud.

Chapter 5

DID YOU KNOW?
THE CAR—A SOLUTION TO POLLUTION

I t's hard to imagine that the automobile (now considered to be a primary source of air pollution) was hailed as the solution to pollution at the turn of the 20th century in New York City. Horse driven traffic in the city had increased. In addition to horse powered buggies that used to take people to and fro, there were horse-pulled trolleys and horse drawn wagons to support a burgeoning economy of the growing city population 1,850,093. There were at least 175,000 horses that traveled the streets or were "parked" at the hitching posts that lined city streets.

It takes very little imagination to picture New York City's early pollution problem. The large amounts of manure had to be shoveled and barged out of the city. It was said that the odor was awful, especially in the summer heat and that the flies were unbearable.

❧

Did you know that what goes around comes around? Ethanol was a primary fuel in the late 1800's and early 1900's. More plentiful than gasoline, many U.S. farmers continued to make their own alcohol fuel from corn stills until Prohibition laws made producing alcohol against the law in 1919.

❧

Did you know that Ford was the first major automobile manufacturer to record a factory recall? It was for an extremely dangerous mistake in manufacturing, possibly deadly, Henry Ford discovered the soft and suppleness of the famous Spanish moss while visiting Savannah, GA. He decided that his cars would only have Savannah's brand of Spanish moss filling the seats of his Model T's. It didn't take long for the company to receive calls from very unhappy customers. Using moss pulled from the trees provides an unexpected little hitch hiker, the "red bug" or "chigger" as we call them. The moss is full of them and every time a grand lady sat on the passengers seat or the master of the plantation was all decked out for a special day, they were more likely to spend the day itching and scratching and since the "red bug" has a habit of seeking dark and moist areas of the body to nest in, scratching that itch was very embarrassing. Ford replaced all of the seats but the stories lasted many years following the recall.

❧

Did you know that Alfred P. Sloan was responsible for the idea of a car manufacturer having a variety of models? His idea was to produce different makes so that a buyer could "move up" if he could afford a more expensive model. He also developed the idea of varying design from model year to model year as well as the three-year cycle of major design changes.

~

Did you know that Ransom E. Olds was the originator of the idea of out-sourcing in the automobile industry? He was the first to design parts for his cars that were manufactured by other companies and then assembled in his plant. He came up with this idea after his plant in Detroit burned down in 1901. In having a number of small companies manufacture some of the parts he needed, he was able to continue production and develop a system of manufacturing that revolutionized the industry. This process is still in use to this day. And two vehicles were named for him the Oldsmobile and REO Speedwagon.

~

Did you know that most American car horns beep in the note F?

~

Did you know that the most dangerous intersection in the U.S. is Flamingo Road and Pines Boulevard in Pembroke Pines, Florida? State Farm Insurance listed this as the Number 1 most dangerous intersection in their latest listing of the worst 10.

The others in order 2-10 are:

- Red Lion Road and Roosevelt Boulevard, Philadelphia, PA;
- Grant Avenue and Roosevelt Boulevard, Philadelphia, PA;
- 7th Street and Bell Drive, Phoenix, AZ;
- 51st Street and Memorial Drive, Tulsa, OK
- 71st Street and Memorial Drive, Tulsa, OK
- 19th Avenue and Northern Avenue, Phoenix, AZ;
- State Highway 121 and Preston Road, Plano, TX;
- Clearview Parkway and Veterans Memorial Boulevard, Metairie, LA
- Fair Oaks Boulevard and Howe Avenue, Sacramento, CA.

Did you know that, in 1905, President Theodore Roosevelt was the first President to ride in a car? However, on his second ride, his chauffeur was stopped for speeding (10 miles an hour). Roosevelt declared he would never ride in a car again. He later ate those words and became both the first President to own a car and the first to drive one.

Did you know that Hiram Johnson was the first political candidate to use a car extensively in his campaign? He was successful in his bid for Governor of California partly because he was able to cover the entire state by car.

Did you know that Clyde Barrow (of Bonnie and Clyde fame) sent a complimentary letter to Henry Ford in 1934 only one month before the shoot-out that took his life? His letter called the Ford a "dandy car" and commented on its operation "...for sustained speed and freedom from trouble, the Ford has got every other car skinned and even if my business hasn't been strictly legal, it doesn't hurt anything to tell you what a fine car you got." The letter is in the Henry Ford Museum at Greenfield Village Dearborn, MI. The car is a part of the Bonnie and Clyde Collection on display in Whiskey Pete's Hotel and Casino 35 miles south of Las Vegas in Primm, NV.

Did you know that there are some strange laws on the books with relationship to driving cars? In California, it is illegal for a woman to drive a car while dressed in a housecoat. In Tennessee, it is illegal to drive a car while sleeping. In New York, it is illegal for a blind person to drive an automobile.

Did you know that in 1900 there were 13 automobile manufacturers in the U.S.? By 1920, that number had grown to 67. By 1925, 5 new manufacturers had opened but 41 had gone out of business. By 1935, only 28 were left. That number dropped to 20 by 1941.

Did you know that automobile windshield wiper was invented by a woman? Mary Anderson thought of and patented the idea for removing snow and ice for streetcars. She was in New York while visiting from her home in Alabama in 1903. The wiper arm was hand operated and the entire mechanism could be removed in the summer since it wasn't being used for removing ice. Also, Henry Ford would postpone the introduction of the 1908 Model T awaiting production. The Model T was the first automobile to use Mrs. Anderson's invention.

∾

Did you know there have been a number of automobiles and trucks that run on wood? Primarily in WWII in Europe, there was a real fuel shortage. The German government and many European citizens developed a method of converting wood to burnable gases. Ford, GM and other companies sold kits that would convert their engines to run on wood. One car with a factory kit would run 100,000 miles.

∾

Did you know that Henry M. Leland, the founder of the Cadillac Company, was the first car manufacturer to build cars with completely interchangeable parts? In 1908, The Royal Automobile Club of Britain supervised the taking apart of the three Cadillac and then reassembled them with a mixture of parts in each car. All three ran perfectly.

Chapter 5

MINE'S BIGGER THAN YOURS!
MINE'S FASTER THAN YOURS!
THE BEGINNING OF AUTOMOBILE RACING

The first recorded race was held in France April 28, 1887. It was organized by a Paris magazine, *Le Velocipede*, as a reliability test. The course was between Neuilly Bridge and Bois de Bouogne a little over a mile. The only competitor, George Bouton won the race.

The first distance race was held in 1894, the course was from Paris to Rouen. The route covered over 79 miles. The first car across the finish line was Bouton's car again. However, it didn't meet the requirements (it needed a stoker and that was against the rules) and was disqualified. The winner Emile Levassor, driving a Panhard-Levassor. The Panhard-Levassor won the next race as well. It was a more traditional race that covered nearly 750 miles from Paris to Bordeaux and back. The winner completed the race in 48 hours with an average speed of 15 mph. He won despite falling asleep on the return leg of the race.

The First Race in the U.S.

The first American automobile race was held on Thanksgiving Day 1895. It was first announced by the Chicago Times-Herald newspaper. Although promoted as a race, it was originated to be a showcase of the kinds of horseless vehicles being made in the US.

The rules for entering were the vehicle had to have at least three wheels and seat at least two people. An umpire was assigned to ride with each entry to make certain that the driver wasn't cheating.

The Illinois countryside was the setting for the 54 miles from Jackson Park in Chicago to Evanston and back. Originally scheduled for the end of October, it had to be postponed because most of the original 89 entries hadn't completed manufacturing their vehicles. The race was rescheduled for November 28th, Thanksgiving Day.

Race day arrived. There was snow on the ground and the temperature was below freezing. Only 6 vehicles show up for the contest. Two were electric cars powered by batteries. There were three gasoline-powered cars built by the German car manufacturer Benz. And, one gasoline-powered car built by the Duryea brothers. It was only the second car the fledgling Duryea brothers had built.

There were many obstacles that faced the competitors. The roads were primitive. The vehicles were unworthy. But it was the weather that played a big part in the Duryea brother's victory. At 8:55 am, the competitors got the "green flag" to start the race. The snow picked up creating slippery roads and the cold temperatures didn't help. Four competitors dropped out. It took Frank Duryea over 10

hours to complete the 54-mile race. He claimed first place with an average speed of 5 miles per hour. The other competitor, in a Benz, developed a severe case of frostbite and finished a full 2 hours later.

Duryea used his $2,000 top prize to start the Duryea Motor Wagon Company and used his worldwide acknowledgement for beating the famous Benz as a promotional reason for buying the Duryea Motor Wagon. In addition to the $2,000, Duryea was awarded the Vanderbilt Cup.

The First Transcontinental Car Race

It was 1905, James Abbott organized the first Transcontinental Race. It was amazing because there was less than 150 miles of paved road in the entire country. The race was more of a staged publicity event than a true contest. Abbott worked for the Department of Public Roads which was a part of the Federal Department of Agriculture. Together with the Olds Motor Works, Abbott advertised for entrants. The top price was $1,000. Strangely enough, the two entrants were a pair of 7-horsepower Curved Dash Olds Runabouts – one called Old Steady, the other called Old Scout.

The race was to follow Lewis and Clark's Oregon Trail from New York to Portland, Oregon. The race started in New York City on May 8th. Old Steady was driven by Percy Megargel and Barton Stanchfield. Old Scout was driven by

Dwight Russ (who was an employee of Olds Motor Works) and Milford Wigle. The race was expected to take 30 days.

All types of natural and unnatural obstacles faced the cars. The excellent racing weather was left in New York and three days into the race it began to rain. It was a rain of biblical proportions.

It rained for three weeks. For over 1,000 miles it was rain, and mud, more mud and more rain. They crossed the Mississippi at Council Bluffs, Iowa. The "roads" were the same trails used by the settlers for 50 years.

AMERICA'S FIRST TRANSCONTINENTAL AUTOMOBILE RACE

Herds of animals blocked the route, availability of gasoline and supplies were scares and maps nonexistent. They reached Cheyenne, Wyoming 11 days behind schedule. Terrain posed the main problem. In Wyoming, Hess wrote in his journal, "we drove 18 hours, forded five streams and traveled a total of 11 miles."

In the Midwest, the drivers encountered a particularly annoying problem. Farmers and ranchers had fenced their land and where ownership crossed the road so did the fences. The drivers decided to simply cut the fences and continue on their way. Badger holes, bent axles, herds of antelopes, bands of wild horses were attracted by the noise the cars made. There were miles of prairie dog towns. The curious prairie dogs would gather at their top of the mounded entrance to their village to observe their alien visitors.

Crossing the Cascade Mountains represented the most difficult challenge to the drivers. Area entrepreneurs had established tool gates at various points along the mountain road. An 8-horse team would cost $4 but hogs were $0.03 a head. The toll guards wanted to charge the cars $4 but the drivers argued that cars were called "road hogs" so they should only pay $0.03 each. A communication from the owner of the toll gate allowed the cars to proceed at no charge.

Old Steady arrived in Portland, Oregon, 44 days after the start. Old Scout arrived 8 days later. Hess was quoted in a Life magazine article as saying, "The truth is we'd all be better off if we never had any danged automobiles…"

Peking to Paris

What is probably the most unusual race ever held was the Peking to Paris race held in 1907. It all started with a newspaper article. The author of a January 1907 article in *Le Martin,* a French newspaper wrote, "…*We ask this question of car manufacturers in France and abroad: Is there anyone who will undertake to travel this summer from Paris to Peking by automobile? Whoever he is, this tough and daring man, whose gallant car will have a dozen nations watching his progress, will certainly deserve to have his name spoken as a byword in the four quarters of the earth…*"

New, unreliable and questionable as a mode of transportation, many considered the new invention little more than a rich man's toy. So the call went out. Would any respond? There were five cars entered—a 15 hp Dutch Spyker, two 10 hp De Dion Boutons, a 6 hp three wheeled Contal and a 40 hp Itala.

In an effort to avoid the heavy rains, the race would start in Peking in May. Crossing a number of mountain ranges and two major deserts weren't the only issues facing the contestants. Poor roads and even the Chinese government represented roadblocks to the racers. The Itala was driven by Prince Scipio Borghese. He spent weeks planning for the trip. He traveled the first 300 miles on horseback before the race. He arranged for extra fuel and parts, which he placed in strategic points along the route. He measured the width of the roads and paths to assure that his Itala could pass.

He ran out of gasoline. He and his co-driver were left stranded. They decided to walk back but had little water. They were found by a band of nomadic Mongolians. The Contal may still be on the side of the road across the Gobi Desert.

Conveniently, telegraph lines crossed the desert. The intrepid racers followed the lines which made the crossing the desert easier than crossing the mountains. It took the Itala four days to cross the Gobi, the others took a half day longer. The Itala was in the lead.

Siberia looked to be easy. The maps showed military roads across the Siberian wilderness. The maps, however, weren't current and did not show that the roads had been abandoned when the Trans-Siberian Railway was built. The roads were washed out in many places, the forest had grown into the roadway and many of the bridges were either in very bad shape or not there at all. The continuing trek across Siberia wasn't without it's close calls. A wreck almost took the Itala and it's drivers out of the competition. However, on July 20th, the Itala drove past a signpost marking the line between Asia and Europe. One week later, the Itala drove into Moscow, a week ahead of schedule and ahead of the rest of the drivers by seventeen days.

The Itala continued with only one issue impeding progress. In Belgium, the Itala was stopped by a policeman for speeding. In responding to a request for his identification, Prince Borghese announced who he was and that "he had just driven from Peking, China." Although the policeman didn't believe the driver's story, confirmation arrived and the Itala was released to proceed.

On August 10th, 1907, only 61 days after the start of the race, the Itala arrived at Paris. The pair of De Dion's arrived 20 days later. The 1907 race has never been duplicated.

Racing in the South

The quality and design of automobiles continued to improve. Race cars began to look less and less like the road cars. By 1948, racing in the southern United States had its own unique look. Often times it was a serious competition of the small business man against the rules of big government. The "moon shine" runner was the rabbit and the hounds were the area police accompanied by revenuers. Many of the better early stock drivers got their training hauling "shine" in

the Carolina mountains. Just ask Junior Johnson.

Southern racing became more organized in 1948. That was the year of the first NASCAR sanctioned race on Daytona beach. Atlanta legend, Red Byron drove his Modified Ford to victory February 21st. In 1949, the series that became the NASCAR Winston Cup started with a race at Daytona, FL and a race at Charlotte, NC.

The Daytona Beach and Road course was somewhat oval-shaped and measured 4.15 miles. The front stretch was a section of Highway A1A. Drivers took a wide corner to enter the beach front and another wide corner would allow them to reenter the highway. 28 cars showed up in Daytona for the first race to win the top prize of $2,000. Over 5,000 people showed up to enjoy the event. Oldsmobile Rocket 88's took the first 4 places and 6 of the vehicles running at the end of the event were Oldsmobile Rocket 88's. An average of 81mph won for it Red Byron. Oldsmobile enjoyed the publicity and Oldsmobile dealers enjoyed brisk sales following the announcement of their success at the race.

In 1951, 54 cars showed up for the Daytona race on the Beach and Road course. In two years the onlookers had more than doubled to 14,000. Driver, local Marshall Teague, took the checkered flag in a Hudson Hornet. 61 drivers showed up for the 1952 event. Daytona is still considered the birthplace of NASCAR racing.

AJ Foyt and Carroll Shelby

Few people could argue that two of the most famous legends in racing history are AJ AJ Foyt and Carroll Shelby. No one has touched Foyt's four Indy 500 wins, his seven Indy Car Championships and he is still the only man to win the Indy 500, Daytona 500 and the 24 Hours of LeMans. AJ won his first midget race at Playland Park in Houston, TX, in 1953. Although he officially retired from racing on May 15th, 1993, Foyt elected to drive two more times – at the inaugural NASCAR Winston Cup race at Indianapolis, August 6th, 1994 and the first NASCAR Craftsman Truck race at Phoenix in 1995. AJ has continued his involvement in the Indy Racing League winning races and championships. Son, Larry Foyt and grandson, AJ Foyt IV currently drives IRL cars.

Carroll Shelby began his career in January of 1952 following a stint in the Air Force. Unlike Foyt, Shelby preferred to compete in straight-line racing. Later that year, Shelby tried his hand at road racing as he took first place in a MG-TC in the MG division and later that day won the Jaguar XK 120 division. Carroll continued his winning ways and

A. J. Foyt

following his championship season in USAC in 1960, his doctor ordered him out of racing in 1961. Shelby began a second successful career at the helm of Shelby-American in March of 1962. Carroll had successfully negotiated to combine a Ford engine with an AC Cars two-seat roadster. The name for the car was revealed to Shelby in a dream. He saw the name Cobra on the front of the car. The rest is history. Shelby has continued to design and manufacturer great American sports cars like the Shelby Mustang, the Dodge Viper and the Shelby Series One, to date.

These two legends would be forever intertwined in 1966 and 1967. Shelby was responsible for the Ford racing program. Henry Ford II decided he wanted Ford back in the forefront of international racing. Shelby-American had been working on a new

Carroll Shelby

Ford, power road race car. What developed was the GT40. In June 1966, with Henry Ford II watching, the three Ford GT40's entered in the 24 Hours of LeMan crossing the finish line 1-2-3. The three cars were built by Shelby-American and Holman-Moody.

The team of Bruce McLaren, Chris Amon, Bob Grossman and Dan Gurney finished first.

Ken Miles, Denny Hulme, Lucien Bianchi, Richard Thompson, Lloyd Ruby and Mark Donohue finished second.

Ronnie Bucknum, Dick Hutcherson, AJ Foyt and Peter Arundell finished third.

It was a clean sweep for the American manufacturer. No one in Europe expected such a performance from the Americans. In 1967, AJ Foyt, Dan Gurney and Bruce McLaren won again for Shelby-American in a Ford GT40.

Chapter 6

21ST CENTURY PHILOSOPHERS
THE LICENSE PLATE WRITERS

t is estimated that there are more than 10 million vanity plates in North America. Through out the US and provinces of Canada, creative geniuses stretch their minds and the combinations of 26 letters of the alphabet, 10 numbers and various punctuation marks to convey a specific message. There are those who's expressed purpose is to get some questionable comment by the powers that be at the DMV. Others write of their passion and their pastimes. Some simply want to gain immortality by placing their name on the bumper of their car for all to see. Modern day puzzlers have found the Vanity Plate writing to be an excellent place to exercise their skills.

What follows is a collection of Vanity Plates. The categories are ones that I found most interesting and represent only a scratch of the surface. I'm sure there are many more on the Internet, if you are interested.

Golf

2BGOLFN (where the driver wants to be)
8 N DER
1 IRON

2 IRON
3 IRON
4 IRON
5 IRON
6 IRON
7 IRON
8 IRON
9 IRON
1 WOOD
2 WOOD
3 WOOD
4 WOOD
5 WOOD
IX IRON
IX FE
5 FE (FE is atomic symbol for iron)
DR GOLF (golf teacher or Dr plays golf)
PAR 3
ILVGLF
T IT UP
PUTN 4DO (a professional golfer who's putting for dough)
G0LFHER
IIIPUTT (nothing to brag about)
EVEN PAR
TEE1UP

Doctors

I had no idea that physicians could be so funny, especially Urologists.

CME2P (probably a Urologist)
2PCME
IP DO U

2TH DR (dentist)
FLOS-M
DOC4JOX (Sports Physician)
HOUSEDR
FOOTSY (podiatrist)
FTFETISH (another podiatrist)
ASSMAN (a proctologist)
CME4DK
CTHRU U (radiologist)
DR IIII (a optometrist)
DRSKULL (neurologist)
ERDOC2B
GONLOCO (at mental hospital)
ICNCYDU (radiologists)
IFXDX (another urologist)
TOOF DR
TZVECL (the 20/20 line on eye chart)
STORK 1 (obstetrician)
STR8NR (orthodontist)
RTROVRS (virologist – retrovirus)
SAY AHH
PP DR (those urologists, funny people)
WE WE DR
OPN WYD
NOPCME (how many ways can those urologists say this)
I SD8EM (anthesiologist)
X-RAY
ITCH DR (dermatologist)
UPP4ME (those hilarious urologists)
XYXX (geneticist)
PKR CKR (another urologist)
RUAJSTED
I TOOTH
OB1GYNOB (Star Wars ob/gyn)

DROFDK (those urologists)
NAPGIVR (anesthesiologist)
DEENSEA
AYE DOK
AR UCNOK
UPP4ME (another Urologist)
KIDZ MD
40WINKS (Sleep DR)
IXMN8U
2020VSN
SORE FT?
DOC TO BE
SAU AHH
A SHRINK
TOOF DR (Dentist)
OB ONE

Celebrities

88 KEYS (Liberace)
A1 AN A2 (Lawrence Welk)
YEHBABY (Tony Little)

On Cars About Cars

Making comments about the vehicles that are licensed is almost as popular and putting people's names on license tags.

FO BY FO (4 wheel drive)
FLEA
ALICE (on a white Rabbit)
IAML8 (on a white Rabbit)
ML8ML8 (on a white Rabbit)
MADHATR

LIA'S JET (on a Jetta)
AHEADAU (on a car in Alabama)
4EN JUNK
4SAFETY (on a Volvo)
SPF 50 (on a convertible)
EATSGAS
FUNFOR2
OBOYMUD
20GS
1OVER0 (infinity on an Infi
ATOYOTA (it's a Palindrome)
BAA BAA (on a Black Jeep)
CANTCME (on a Dodge Stealth)
DE SADE (on a Mercury Marquis)
EGOTAG (on a BMW)
FE2O3 (iron oxide - on a rusty old truck)
GROWL (on a Jag)
HAMACHI (Yellow Tail in a sushi bar—on a yellow Porsche 911SC)
HAUDI (on an Audi)
HSSSS (on a Shelby Cobra Mustang)
HUM THIS (on a Hummer in Colorado)
TWEETY (on a yellow 57 Thunderbird)
TENGO 2 (Spanish for "I Have 2")
SLYASA (sly as a … on a Audi Fox)
SOL MAN (on a Honda del Sol)
PRRRRR (on a Jaguar)
IX (on a Jaguar IX but in pre-classical Mayan ix was Jaguar)
IXIVIV (on a Porsche 944)
IXXI (on a Porsche 911)
IX XIV (on a Porsche 914)
IXIIIX (on a Mazda 929)
VOMET (1965 Comet)
BLUCANDY (on a blue tricked out import)

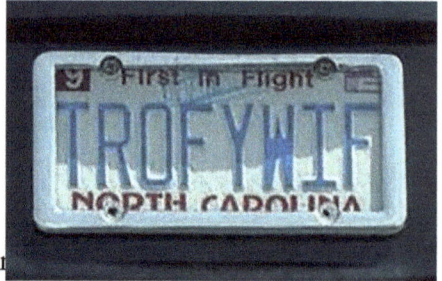

ALL RISE (on a 1968 GTO Judge)
LIKEAROC (Chevy truck)
RDBOWTI (Chevy Monte Carlo)
NOBOWTIE (on a Mustang)
GOT RICE (Supercharged Honda – rice burner)
RIBBIT (on a bright green Honda del Sol that looked like a frog)
CREEPERS (on a jeep - Jeepers Creepers)
NUKE GM
OJ REPO (on a white Bronco)
AU RINGS (Audi – au symbol for gold)
CALMB4 (on a Geo Storm)
Y2KBUG (2000 VW Beetle)
EXPLORN (on a Ford Explorer)
N2ORBIT (on a Saturn)
6 ROCK (also on a Saturn)
WEBS (on a Spyder)
ITCBITC (on a Spyder – Itsy Bitsy Spider)
VRM VRM
FORDY-7 (on a 1947 Ford)
SEEUSA (on a 1957 Chevy)
GIDIUP (on a ford Mustang)
BEAM HER (on a BMW)
BAD 88
SNAAB
SOUXZNS
JESBUGN (on a VW)
MYXCAPE
KEMO SAAB
BEHEMTH (on a Suburban)
BOXLUNCH (on an Element)
LE BMER
MAS DA
SKY DYE (on a blue car)
LE TAG (on a Le Car)

U G L Y (old snow removal truck)
ITSAJETTA
LEMON
19 6T5
LICENSE
MY CAR
RUN DMC
L JEEPO
NOT OJ (on a white Bronco)
1OVER0 (on an Infinity)
WASCALY (on a Rabbit)
SKUNK (black car, white strip)
SALTBOX (on a white Honda Element)
JACKNBOX (on a van, driver Jacl?)

I Got It By The DMV

3M TA3 (mirror image - read it backward)
9INPNS
38DDD
38-24-34
1000101 (binary for 69)
DMV SUX (Someone wasn't thinking.)
DREK (Ask someone who speaks Yiddish.)
EM KNAPS (another mirror image)
GOVT SUX (A VA judge ruled that DMV had to give this plate
to the vehicle owner)
HARDICK (on a construction truck with Hardick Construction
on the side)
IM1RU2 (the gay community represented)
SRUOY PU (one more mirror image)
NO CACA
WANTSOM?
MSAGRO (spell backward)

DOOBIE
POOHEAD
WOODI
DOGEDO
MOO POO

Geeks

8BIT ME (8 bits = a byte)
ID-BUGM (system analyst)
2B OR D5 (a programmer's joke)
IDOCPUS (computer tech)
IMA NERD
SU ROOT (SuperUser Root - a Unix geek)
THX JAVA
MACGEEK
MACMYDAY
MAC-USER
UNIXINU
LIV2HAK
DOT COM
NETGEEK
WWWGEEK
HTML KID
GEEK1
CHKDSK (check disc)
MACGEEK
MP3

Educators

MBA@DUKE (a young woman in NC)
IMA PHD
PHLOSFR

BUGDOC (a PHD in entomology)
I IS PHD (hopefully not in English)
I M N MBA (student at Harvard)
DEUS 777
EDUC8T
IEDUC8M (high school teacher)
PROF (university professor)
FIZXPHD (PHD in Physics)
ABC-4U (kindergarten teacher)
COOPR8 (cooperative learning teacher)
2N2 R4
EDUK8OR

Intellectuals

0GRAVITY
WHENRWE
MD MD (It's a paradox.)
OXY MRN
BI POLAR
AG HG (on a silver Mercury – ag is the symbol for silver, hg for mercury)
IAM ALF (ALF or Alien Life Form.)
C9H13N (chemical label for amphetamine)
UBU IBI
ALLMAYA (MAYA is ILLUSION in Sanskrit. Everything is illusion)
4XX 4XY (4 boys & 4 girls big family van)
2BORWAT (Hamlet)
KUZIKN
I THINK
AD HOC
CARPADM
CZTHEDY

ITHINK2
AS IF
INNATE
4SHADOW
KPASAMD (what's up doc?)
I AM UR
NCC1702
XNTRIC
MYSNCAN (sn symbol for tin)
NO IDEA
MAKETSO
Y YNOT
PHOXIE
YWORY
Q AND A
EPICURE
YYYYY
WARP1
PROGENY
E EQ MCC
ID EGO
GU10TAG (Guten Tag is German for good day – on a Mercedes Benz.)
HIHO AG (ag is the symbol for Silver)
KEMO SAAB (on a Saab 900E)
SQLAPS (Aesculapius is the Roman God of Healing – maybe he's a doctor.)
PH 7 (the "neutral" guy at the lab)
NACL H2O (nacl is the symbol for sodium chloride – salt so, salt water)
REDSHFT (In a Doppler Shift as something moving away at high speeds)
QUICK AG (ag symbol for silver)
RIEN DE 9 (French "nothing's new" why? QUOI DE 9 ("what's

new" in French)

1 PB FOOT (pb is symbol for lead - 1 lead foot)

FE CITY (fe is symbol for iron – owner from Pittsburgh or he likes the beer)

AG BULL (ag is symbol for Silver - on a silver Taurus)

XXIVKTAU (au is symbol for gold. Roman numerals XXIV is 24 - 24 karat gold)

ILITRIT (illiterate)

QETESH (Egyptian/Syrian goddess of love and beauty – female driving)

JEENYUS

EIEIO

TMBUC2

IN4RED

Vocations & Avocations

KAR DOK (mechanic)

PHILOSFR

TAX ATTY

IGOEVA (astronaut – eva is extra-vehicular activity)

RX CIST (pharmacist)

SHO FIR (chauffeur)

LENSMAN

4CASTR (weather man)

ARTIST 1

CALQL8 (auditor)

CME4PIPE (plumber)

CRIMPAYS (attorney's Porsche 911)

DJ4FEE (want to dance)

ICU 121 (optometrist)

CYCOPTH (Is that a profession?)

DRG DLR (on a car at pharmacy)

ESQUIRE (attorney)

FAMFIXR (family therapist)
VIZUAL
GR8BUNS (on a bakery van.)
H8 PEPZ (on a Coca Cola Van)
HIFEES (lawyers car, what else)
HOOCH (car outside liquor store)
HUT ONE (football player's car.)
IEATFIRE (fireman)
I FLYHI (flight attendant)
I INSUR (insurance sales person)
IKNEADU (massage therapist)
INFL8 (hot air balloonist)
INS BZ (insurance agent)
STOS UP (investment broker)
SHOOTER (member of a rifle team)
RURT2 (Are you arty, too? gallery owner)
PILPUSR (pharmacist – pill pusher)
POMPOMS (former cheerleader)
PRAY (on a priest's van)
PUCK U (hockey coach)
OBSERV1 (astronomer)
PAID2RGU (attorney)
NUNSRUS (on a van full of sisters)
NOETHICS (attorney)
MY FEE (on a red Mercedes convertible)
N2SHEEP (a rancher's car)
MAKMLAF (Las Vegas comedian)
MOVN FR8 (trucking co dispatcher)
IRESCU (EMT on a rescue squad)
ISUE4U (another attorney)
I THINK (Director of the Center for Creative Thinking)
ITHINK2 (wife of the above)
ITOETAG (coroner)
JETJOCK (fighter pilot)

KILDUMP (high school baseball umpire)
LITIG8 (car driven by an attorney)
LOXMIF (lock smith)
LV 2 TCH (teacher)
RD DR (road doctor)
USA2DA (a USAToday employee)
W8LFTR (weightlifter)
WEASL 1
XY RN (a male registered nurse's car)
XCAV8 (on a construction truck)
HAIR DR (hair stylist)
ORD ONE (chief or Chicago's O'Hare airport - airport indicator is ORD)
DOLLS4U (a Doll Store owner)
BYTE LAW (attorney specializing in software law)
MIS&ACCT
I DENY U (banker)
8X A MOM
ISOLDIT (realtor)
MSHONCHO (the woman in charge)
HAER4YOU (owner of a hearing center)
NEWZPIX (newspaper photojournalist)
SNAP 2 (photographer)
SMOKINN (volunteer firefighter)
HOSER (automotive hose salesman)
SK8HARD (hockey player)
4ENSIX (forensics tech)
TO-FROM (transportation service)
THE REV
BEV MD (bartender)
DOGTOR (vet)
FIXNFLY (airplane mechanic)
WE SAW (private investigator)
IMCOOKN (chef)

AIRHED (director of the New Hampshire air pollution agency)
GENER8 (control operator in a power station)
ISUEDRS (attorney with a specialty)
MOO U2 (dairy farmers)
HITMIX (DJ)
CUFF EM (police officer)
DAWG LB (animal control officer)
DENTFXR (car body shop owner)
DR PYRO (fireworks researcher)
DUZ HAIR (beautician)
ILAYPYPE (plumber)
727CAPT (airline pilot)
90 PLUS (minor league pitcher whose fast ball is consistently above 90 MPH)
GO2JAIL (director of Christian prison ministries – looking for volunteers)
MYOFFICE (traveling salesman)
NOPITY (police officer)
TATERMAN (potato farmer)
CARDMAN (baseball card collector)
GOTCHA (security officer)
IDYE4U (beautician)
EMCEE (professional speaker)
BY&SELL (realtor)
DOG&BRAT (hotdog business or a family with a dog and kid)
LUV2SKI2
TUNANUT
DOCROCK!
MLS2GO
ADS-PLUS
SPIN DR
PIT CRU
HEAR4YOU (@ a hearing clinic)
DRHAPPY

REALIST8
LV 2 TCH
THERA P
WALL $T
COPPER
MEE D8R
ANEWBIS
#1TRAINR
NOETHICS (lawyer)
WEBMSTR
SHOOTER (rifle team)
NEWS DOG
TOONS (cartoonist)
ANACTOR
ART PROF
WHO PHD
BACRUB?
LACT 8
ERNURSE
LAWYR2B
16 APR (accountant)
24 KT(jeweler)
2BOR?

Hearse Humor

U2 1 DAY
STIF ONE
THE END
RU NEXT
NEXT
M BALMED
ITSTIME
RM41MR (Room for one more)

WEDIG4U
U21DAY
I BURY
DIGINIT
LSTRIDE
YERNXT

Music

B SHARP
BESHARP
B FLAT
FUGUE (on a Honda PRELUDE)
UKULELE T42 24T (a song)
A SAXIST
BCDDCBA (musical notes in the forth movement of Beethoven's
Ninth)
INGFLAT (composer)
SAXUAL (sax player)
MINUET (musician)
BASOON
MOZART
SONATA
BACHATU

Spiritual

B LIEVE
1WTHGOD
PSALM66
REACHOUT
GODSAVEZ
GODZGOOD
I FND IT

RU4GOD
LUKE4 8 ("Get thee behind me Satan")
YESLORD
YME GOD (a perpetual question)
PR8SHM
I4ANI
WELL-ONE
TESTIFY1
REACHOUT
RU SAVED
UR LOVED
PRO JESUS
FR ABOVE
YES LORD
H2O WALKR
JOHN II
THKUFTHR
RUN 2 HM

Puzzles

IRIGHTI (right between the eyes)
ISHOTI (shot between the eyes)
MILL1ON (one in a million)
14ALL41

Humorous

HAHAHA
WHUT?
GO SHAGIN (That's dancing in the Southern US, it's different
in the UK)
DOG8IT (homework)
PICADILY (a VW with a US & British flag)

NO-9TO5 (on his own)

I (one of the best I found)

PA6-5K (Pennsylvania 6-5000 1940's song)

GGGGGGG (G-string)

KILLSHOT (a racket ball player)

DOODY (on an Audi - Audi Doody)

1DN1TGO (one daughter graduated and married, one more at home)

CH-CHING

WONGWAY

DA WABIT (on a VW Rabbit)

WASCALY (on a wescally Rabbit)

E FUDD

TAGURIT

4 LABS

3BLONDS

XRATED

NYC4LIFE

SWEETER

COKE (on a DeLorean)

BIPOLAR

BS MAN

BIGOT

IGOT 2P

PMS ESP (The owner says it means "bitch that knows everything.")

PMSX365 (all year long)

NOT YOU (On a PA tag where the motto is "you have a friend in PA.")

N ROLL (on an IROC Z-28 – IROC N ROLL)

MY MINK

MEANMY (on a Dodge Shadow – Me and My Shadow)

MAFIA (stretch Black Limo)

QT PI (Cutie Pie)

UUUD444 (Use the force, Luke)

BEE BOP (on a 1956 Hot Rod)
FINSUP (Parrothead)
ZPDDODA (Zip a dee do dah)
POLLACK (the license plate was on upside down)
FE FIST (fe is symbol for iron)
0 2L84T (on a car with a British flag – so "naught (not) too late for tea")
EEYORE (seen near Pooh corner)
1NYQTPIE
4 BIRDS
HARD H2O
SUZ-U-LUZ
DANG-MAN
ME-OO-MY
NO CACA
&DEE
PAPPY
OB1KANOB
LOVIN U2
"MUMZY"
EXNTRIK
CYNCITY (in Las Vegas)
MOJO
BUBBALA
YY2WRY (too wise and too weary)
CCCCOLD (VT plate)

Trying To Hard

T G I F
WUTEVR
FIDL DD (Gone with the Wind)
H2O GATE (G. Gordon Liddy's plate on his Corvette)
ICUUQTU (I see you, you cutie you.)

IAMYY4U (I'm too wise for you – really)
ILOVEME (the perfect vanity plate)
VANITY (that's right)
PONOMO (a Cadillac in GA)
OJDIDIT
PARDONME
PATTY POO
1BIGMAC
PB4 UGO (a minivan packed with kids)
NYUKX3 (must have been a Stooges fan – nyuk, nyuk, nyuk)
MY CAR
4EVER29
MR QUICK
ITSADUK
ITSPHY6 (It's physics.)
JEALOUS
JK MNO (no L or Noel)
KEPT (on a Rolls-Royce Corniche driven by a beautiful woman)
KIDBGON (red BMW with middle aged couple)
REVO EVOM (reads MOVE OVER in a mirror)
VAN GO
WHAT COP (on an RX7)
WD XXXX (WD40)
DRS BABE
RUH ROH (scooby Doo)
SEEK 2XL
GOT2SWET
HIHOWRU
ME2ME2
DEJA VU
LOSTTAG
YOYOMOM
ETGOHOM
HOOWAH

Ralph Jarrells

NDNGIRL
EXUZ ME
TEX SEZ
WHOHAW
SOBOSOB (son of a son of a bitch)
OMYWORD
INA SNIT
CPTNEMO
GUNG HO
BOYOBOY
ACHTUNG

Chapter 7

ROAD SIDE ATTRACTIONS
&
HIGHWAY ADVERTISING

I n the beginning, the car was an oddity that would draw attention to itself. As a matter of fact, P.T. Barnum drew crowds with a new car as a sideshow attraction in his circus in 1896. The car manufactured by the Duryea brothers received top billing over the giant, the fat lady and the elephant.

As more cars hit the road, the car it self was a roadside attraction. At the turn of the 20th century, drive a new vehicle into almost any town in the country and you would draw a crowd. In 1900, there were 13 manufacturers in the U.S. Along with name you would recognize such as the Oldsmobile and the Packard, there were the Autocar, the Baker Electric, the Columbia, the Haynes-Apperson, the Locomobile, the Stanley Steamer, the Sternes, the Waverly Electric, the White Steamer and the Winton that didn't pass the test of time.

Between 1901 and 1920, the number of automobile manufacturers grew to 67. When was the last time you saw an Allen or a Chalmers, a Dort or a Columbia, a King or a Jordan, a Jackson or a K-R-I-T, a Moon or a Templar and who could forget the ever popular Grant. Yes, they all were makes of cars in the 20 years that followed the

turn of the century. But, by 1941 they were all a thing of the past as the number of manufacturers had decreased to 20. A number of early ads follow.

First came the car, then...

The advent of the car spawned many allied industries most of which had nothing to do with the vehicles. Motels, drive-in restaurants, drive-in movies, the list goes on. True, the availability of a car provided the means for many more people to experience the wonders and beauties of our country. Being able to see natural attractions like the Grand Canyon, the Painted Desert, the Redwood Forest, the Mississippi River, the Atlantic and Pacific Oceans, the Rocky Mountains, all in one lifetime was made possible by the car and the national road system. The opportunity to see and experience the important locations of the country's history was made available to vast numbers of people, as well. But, the car and road systems made seeing other things possible – things like "road side attractions" and highway advertising.

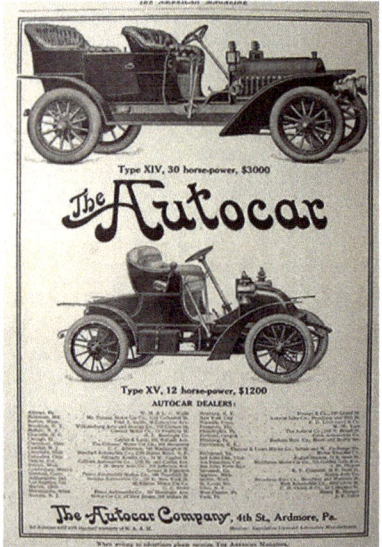

When I first started researching the topic of Roadside Attractions, I started with the assumption that Florida and California would be the location of the majority of these phenomena. How wrong that assumption was.

The signature line from the movie Field of Dreams, "Build it and they will come", is certainly true of Road Side Attractions. Whether it is See Live Alligators, Orange Juice "all you can drink", Mystery Hill, religious shrines, petting zoos, fire works stands, live caged bears, the world's largest ball of twine, and this list also goes on, and on. Even some of the last vestiges of the once powerful passenger railway system were relegated to nothing more than a ride in a roadside attraction.

Not only could you see the wonderful and beautiful and the historical, you could see the bizarre, the unusual, the fake and lots of other useless, unnecessary and pointless. And, you were provided the opportunity to buy a seemingly endless selection of souvenirs.

Salt and pepper shakers, ashtrays, novelties, post cards (for those who wanted to brag to their friends and family of their travels – no matter how inane or ridicules). Toys, hand crafted "art" and international offerings from Japan, Mexico and, more recently, for any number of emerging countries made up what represented row upon row of displays in the attractions.

Not to be outdone by these "johnnie come lately" merchants, the growing numbers of people driving on road trips became the focus of marketing efforts of regular merchants. Outdoor advertising was born. 1867 is the earliest record of real estate being leased for billboard advertising. As prices for the billboards increased, innovative marketers became more and more creative in their efforts to promote their products and locations. Burma Shave and their roadside poetry is probably the best known (more about Burma Shave later in this chapter). But there are numerous examples, some being very creative.

The roadside attraction

mentality was adopted by local businesses and it could be said that some of them took it to extremes. Building their buildings like a tea pot or other shapes that typified their business and putting a three dimensional do-nut or other symbol on top of the building were ways used to blend a business with the marketing philosophy of the road side attraction..

As the numbers of the motoring public grew, the size, services and selection of the road side attractions grew resulting in legitimate businesses that catered to these motorists. Motel chains, multi-location restaurants and gasoline stations were at the top of this growth. Consider that Disney Land, Disney World, Sea World and Universal Theme parks are little more than a sophisticated amalgamation of See Live Alligators, orange juice "all you can drink", unique exhibits, ride our train and buy our souvenirs.

See Rock City

Did you know that one of the most successful roadside advertising programs was the "See Rock City" campaign. The "See 7 States from Rock City" claim may have drawn multiple thousands of visitors but it was the unique advertising vehicle that caught their attention. Large white letters on a black background painted on the sides and roofs of barns and other buildings was the genius behind the success of Rock City. Ultimately there were 900 barns, general stores and other large buildings that called to the motoring public to visit Rock City atop Lookout Mountain just outside Chattanooga, Tennessee.

Rock City was the brain child of Garnet and Frieda Carter. The gardens they planted and the view were spectacular but it was Frieda Carter's long time interest in European folklore that provided the central theme as a Fairyland. Fresh from their success in opening and franchising

the first miniature golf course, Tom Thumb Golf, the Carters set out to develop some 700 acres at the top of Lookout Mountain. Utilizing naturally occurring rock outcroppings and a collection of imported German statues of gnomes and fairy characters, the gardens were initially for their own benefit.

It was Garnet who first realized that lots of people would be willing to pay to see this unique development. Rock City opened May 21, 1932. The people did come but not in the numbers the Carter's had hopped. Since Rock City was off the beaten paths, Carter had to establish the desire to go to Rock City before the potential visitor was anywhere near. Carter's idea is now a part of advertising history.

Carter enlisted the help of Clark Byers, a young sign painter, to travel all over the nation. He would offer to paint a farmer's barn or other prominent building for free if he would allow the slogan, "See Rock City" to be painted where it was obvious from the highway. Starting in 1936, Byers painted 900 structures from Michigan to Texas. Did you know that you can still See Rock City? It is operated by the third generation of Garnet and Frieda. Did you know you can take a bird house home with the legendary "See Rock City" paint scheme?

Howard Johnson - 28 Flavors

It was 1925. Howard Deering Johnson was 27, he had borrowed $500 to purchase a small patent medicine store with a soda fountain that sold newspapers in Wollaston, a section of Quincy MA, following his father's death. Since he had assumed his father's debt, he found he was $40,000 in the red. He knew he had to do

71

something different. His first idea was to sell newspapers on the corner in nearby communities. It was successful but he isn't famous for developing the idea of news boys.

The store sold ice cream – vanilla, chocolate and strawberry. His ice cream was pretty much the same as every other soda fountain. He believed the secret to future success was to expand the selection of flavors but he also wanted people to talk about how good his ice cream was. So he began to experiment with his recipe. After a number of efforts with the hand cranked freezer in the basement of his store, he settles on two things that had improved the flavor of his ice cream – doubling the butterfat content and using only natural flavors. He began expanding the flavor selection and by 1935 Howard Johnson's offered 28 flavors.

His changes were successful and he had people standing in lines outside of the first Howard Johnson's for his ice cream. Expansion was the answer. Howard Johnson's ice cream was available at stands at nearby beaches and soon at other locations. In three years he had paid off all of the debt and set the stage for further expansion.

He decided to offer hot dogs, hamburgers and other easily prepared food. But, quality was the key in each addition. His "drug" store with a soda fountain had become a restaurant and Howard Johnson's was on its way.

In 1929, a second location with a broader menu was opened in downtown Quincy. Johnson had envisioned a chain of restaurants that would have the confidence of travelers. He saw the success of his restaurants tied to the automobile which he saw changing the face of America. This along with better roads and his belief that more people would be traveling and they would want good food and sensible prices. The second store had left Johnson borrowed to the limit so his expansion plans were on hold.

It was then he conceived the idea of franchising. He convinced a Cape Cod restaurant owner to put Howard Johnson's name on his restaurant for a fee and buy food and supplies from him. The idea worked for both men and by 1935 the Howard Johnson's name was on 35 restaurants that featured Johnson's ice cream. By 1940 there were 100 Howard Johnson's restaurants along the Atlantic coast.

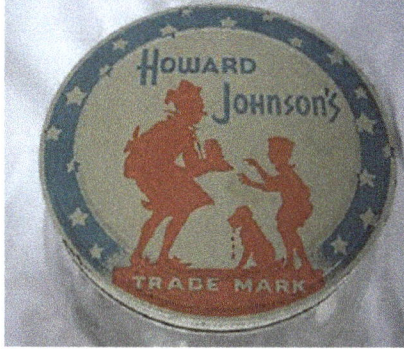

It isn't recorded when the bright orange roof became a fixture on the restaurants but it was certainly the predecessor of those arches and other road side attractors that are an integral part of franchise food places.

In 1940, Howard Johnson's became the first turnpike restaurant by opening its location on the Pennsylvania Turnpike. In 1954, the company ventured into the franchise motor lodge business with a location in Savannah, GA/ In 1961, Howard Johnson's became a public company. By the late 1970's the company had grown to over 1,000 restaurants and over 500 motor lodges. Competition from franchise food chains and hotel/motel chains began to erode Howard Johnson's foot hold in the marketplace and in 1980 a British conglomerate, the Imperial Group bought the company for more than $630 million.

There are few remnants of the company left. However, all 28 flavors made from the original recipe are still available at other restaurants and ice cream shops thanks to a bulk packaging agreement with The Ice Cream Club of Boynton Beach, FL.

Burma Shave

Ask anyone who was old enough to read in the '30's, '40's or '50's about Burma Shave and they will tell you the story of the roadside slogans that were all over the country. They may not know much about the product but they are likely to remember the 6 signs about 100 feet apart. *"His beard was long and strong and tough. He lost his chicken in the rough. Burma-Shave"*

It was the advertising brainchild of Allan Odell. Allan reportedly saw four hand lettered signs along the road in 1926 advertising a gas station's restrooms and other services. It started him wondering if the idea would work for his father's company. It took $200 in scrap lumber; Allan and his brother Leonard created the first Burma-Shave signs and placed them along Route 35 between Albert Lea and Minneapolis, Minnesota. Within weeks of the installation of the first set of signs, drug stores were sold out of Burma-Shave

HER CHARIOT	A MAN A MISS
RACED 80 PER	A CAR - A CURVE
THEY HAULED AWAY	HE KISSED THE MISS
WHAT HAD	AND MISSED
BEN HUR	THE CURVE
Burma Shave	*Burma Shave*

and ordering more. A year later, Allan and Leonard had installed more signs throughout Minnesota and part of Wisconsin. They spent $25,000 on signs and sales hit $68,000. *"A Man A Miss A Car A Curve He kissed the Miss and Missed the Curve. Burma-Shave"*

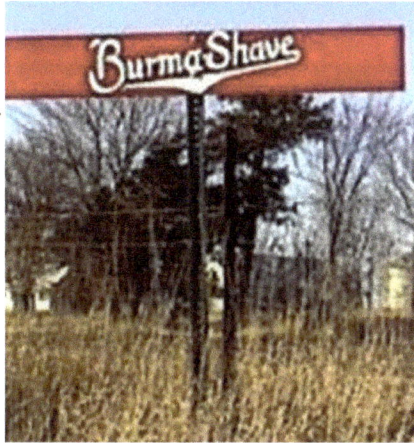

Burma-Shave was the first brushless shaving cream. It was ideal for the mobile American man. He didn't have to pack his wet shaving brush and cup. It was a new concept and the new advertising campaign was a hit as well. *"Dinah Doesn't Treat Him Right but If He'd Shave, Dinah-Mite. Burma-Shave"*

Allan wrote most of the early sign jingles. But, a lot of the success of the program was when the company offered prizes up to $100 for jingles submitted by customers. *"Before I Tried It The Kisses Missed But Afterward Boy! The Misses Kissed. Burma-Shave"*

At its most successful, there were some 7,000 jingles in 45 states. They were maintained by just 8 sign trucks. The sign crews called themselves PHD's – post hole diggers. The jingles were changed at least once a year. Unlike today's outdoor billboards, most of the land owners (mostly farmers) allowed the Burma-Shave sign installation for a case of product a year. *"If You Think She Likes Your Bristles Walk Barefooted Through Some Thistles. Burma-Shave"*

Burma-Shave had grown to $3 million in sales. In the early '60's, the Odell family sold the company to Gillette which became a part of the American Safety Razor Company and later a part of Phillip Morris. These much larger companies thought the jingles were a silly idea and moved their advertising to other media, primarily television. By 1966, the only Burma-Shave signs you could find were in museums and private collections. *"Said Farmer Brown Who's Bald On Top "Wish I Could Rotate The Crop." Burma-Shave"*

Clifton Odell, founder of Burma-Shave died in 1958. Allan Odell the originator of the sign idea died in 1994. His Brother, Leonard, died in 1991.

"Don't Pass Cars On Curve Or Hill If The Cops Don't Get You Morticians Will"

Other Roadside Attractions

You'll find the famous and infamous roadside attractions throughout the United States, in communities large and small. Nebraska's largest ball of stamps is at Boy's Town. Lucy the elephant hotel is in Margate, NJ. Prairie Dog town is in Oakley, KS right next door to the world's largest ice cream cone. In Colorado you can find the "Famous Miracle House" in Manitou Springs where optical illusions leave you questioning what you see and the Prostitution Museum in Cripple Creek where children under 10 get in free.

Here's a list of some of the most unusual:

- The World's Largest Cat in Jersey City, NJ
- The World's Largest Tire in Allan Park, MI
- The World's Largest Goose in Sumer, MO
- The World's Largest Thermometer in Baker, CA
- The World's Largest Egg in Winlock, WA
- The World's Largest Lemon in Lemon Grove, CA and
- The World's Largest Ball of Twine in Cawker City, KS

Which has always begged the question, who authenticates the "World's Largest" claim?

Let's not forget

- The Unrequited Love Carvings in Waxahachie, TX
- The Concrete Outling of the USS South Dakota in Sioux Falls, SD
- The Dog Chapel in St. Johnsbury, VT
- The Oldest Concrete Street in America in Bellefontaine, OH

- The Scale Model of the Solar System in Peoria, IL
- Dick & Jane's Spot in Ellensburg, WA
- McDonald's Store #1, Des Plaines, IL
- The Hippie Memorial in Arcola, IL
- The 1st Wendy's restaurant Columbus, OH
- The Passenger Pigeon Memorial Hut in Cincinnati, OH
- The Tower of Wooden Pallets in Sherman Oaks, CA
- The Town That Time Forgot, Glasgow, VA
- The World's Smallest Church Oneida, NY
- The Lord's Prayer Rock in Bristol, VT and
- The World's Largest Mary Statue Windsor, OH
- There's even an Eiffel Tower replica in Paris, TN

These "sideshows of the highway" live up to their namesake. Nothing is too bizarre to become another roadside attraction (apologies to Tom Robbins). Evidence of this is the Blessed Virgin Mary in a Stump (Salt Lake City, UT), the only survivor of the Battle of Little Bighorn (a horse named Comanche) is stuffed and on display (Lawrence, KS) and the Witchcraft Museum (New Orleans, LA). However, what is arguably the biggest roadside attraction of all, is an entire town—Las Vegas.

Thanks to the magic of lights and plastic, you can make a single trip and visit dozens of the world's great cities and live like many of your favorite legendary characters. Where else can you be in New York, Paris, Venice and the land of the Pharaohs all within one evening. You attend a circus, visit a tropical garden or an underwater wonderland, watch a volcano erupt and participate in a medieval dinner while cheering on your favorite knight. Where else can you see old masters' art, world famous musical stars, million dollar automobiles

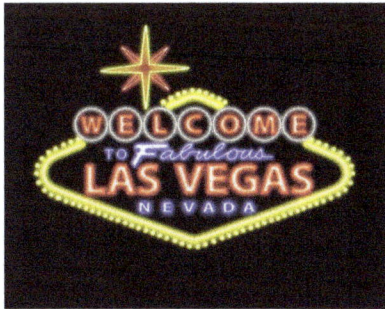

and almost anything you can imagine. Only Las Vegas, and remember "What happens in Las Vegas, stays in Las Vegas."

Chapter 8

FIRST CAME THE CAR
PART 2

A s with most life changing inventions, the car changed the way our parents and grand parents did almost everything. New business categories were created to cater to a new generation of mobile citizens. Businesses were developed to handle the needs of the drivers and passengers. A country on wheels represented unlimited opportunity. Motels, drive-in restaurants, drive-in theaters and car care along with the more unusual such as drive-in churches, drive-in funeral homes and the joke of a drive-in confessional called "toot and tell."

The Motor Hotel—Motel

Although there may be some arguments about when the "first" motel, The Savvy Traveler says it was the Milestone in San Luis Obispo, CA, located halfway between San Francisco and Los Angeles.

You might imagine that this new concept in over-nighting would have originated in California.

In 1925, L.A. architect, Arthur Heinemen built the Milestone. The original building stands only a few feet from highway 101, now a super-highway. It is currently under renovation by current owner Bob Davis who also owns the upscale next door neighbor, the Apple Farm Inn.

The Milestone's restaurant looked like a Spanish Mission. In 1925, you could get a two-room suite with kitchen and a garage for $1.25 per night. Early advertising claimed, "The skies are clear, the air tingles and you never saw such a blue ocean." These early resorts offered to augment the adventure and romance of travel and the open road.

Heineman had a dream of building motels like the Milestone "like a string of pearls from Seattle to L.A." The Great Depression put an end to his dream. Twenty years later, Holiday Inn took up where Heineman left off.

The Drive-In Restaurant

The very first Drive-In restaurant is up for grabs. One source claims that the first "drive-in concept restaurant" where people were served their food in their cars opened in Glendale, CA in 1936.

Another source credits Texan J.G. Kirby with opening the first drive-in restaurant in 1921. The Pig Stand, a barbecue restaurant, was located on the Dallas-Fort Worth Highway.

Arguably, the first drive-in restaurant could have been the first A & W Root Beer stand opened by Roy Allen in June of 1919 in Lodi,

CA. In 1920, Allen opened his second stand in Sacramento. It was the Sacramento location that first offered "tray boys" providing curb side service. In 1922, Allen partnered with Frank Wright, one of his original employees in Lodi. The company name was established by combining their initials "A" for Allen and "W" for Wright. In 1924, Allen began to actively pursue franchising his A & W Root Beer restaurants. By 1933, Allen had 17 franchised locations in the west and mid-west. By 1950 there were 450 A & W locations and there were 2,000 in 1960. There were a number of ownership changes in the '70's, '80's and '90's but A & W restaurants are still available throughout the country.

The prevalent 21st century version of the drive-in restaurant has lost most of its personal contact. Placing an order through an electronic circuit as you drive through a line that circles the establishment has little of the charm of the early drive-ins. Sonic is the only chain that I know of that has kept the curbside contact of the '50's. Most towns have one or two locally owned drive-in restaurants that have tenaciously hung on to their niche. To these hardy souls I say, "thank you."

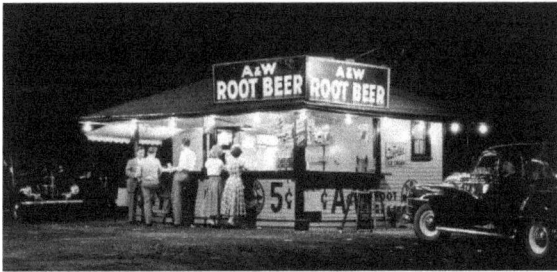

The Drive-In Theater

As indicated in Chapter 2, the first drive-in theater opened in Camden, NJ, on June 6, 1933. A fee of $.25 per car and $.25 per person was charged to see Adolphe Menjou star in the movie "Wife Beware." The idea was that of Richard Hollingshead, a young sales manager for his father's Auto Parts store. Richard wanted to combine his two favorite interests, movies and cars. He received US Patent #1,909,537 for the Drive-In Theater, which was issued in May of

1933. In May, 1950, his patent was declared invalid.

As with many young inventors, his home became his laboratory. His first effort was somewhat primitive. Utilizing a 1928 model Kodak projector that he mounted on the hood of his car, he projected the film on a sheet nailed to trees in his backyard. He used his driveway to experiment on parking. Cars in a line experienced difficulty in seeing the movie. It was great for the first car but the others' line of sight were blocked. He finally found the proper spacing for the cars.

With an investment of $30,000 Hollingshead constructed the first Drive-In Theater on Crescent Boulevard in Camden, NJ.

Hollingshead's idea grew to a full fledged industry with over 5,000 drive-in theaters in operation by World War II. With gas rationing and so many American service men and women overseas, the war years called a halt to the industry's growth.

With the development and wide spread acceptance of home video

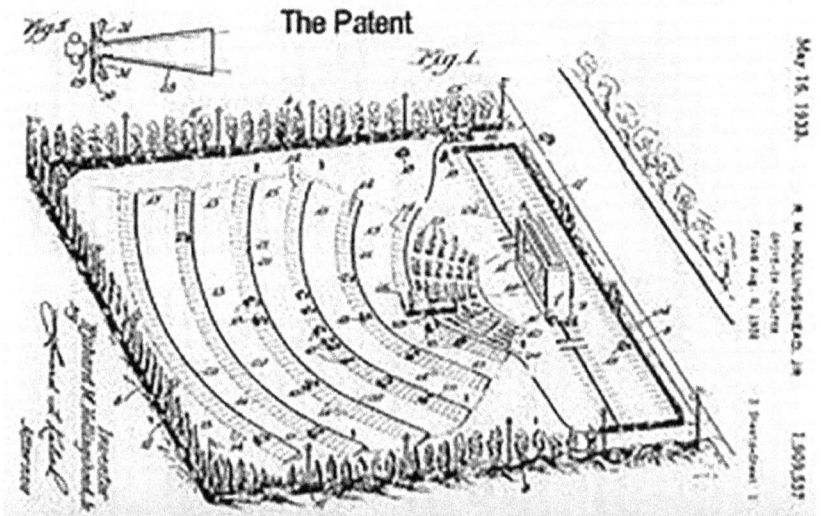

The Patent

and cable television, the drive-in theater was destined to a place in history. There are fewer than 100 left in the U.S.

The drive-in theater craze spawned the development of the movie industry and provided an outlet for low budget action, drama and horror pictures called B movies. Low budget productions required locations outside of Hollywood. Movie production companies like Earl Owensby Studios, Shelby, NC were key in providing movies such as Dark Sunday, Damon's Law, Rottweiler, Buckstone County Prison, Chain Gang and Death Driver (most of which Earl Owensby starred in) for drive-in theaters.

By the way, the largest drive-in theater was in Copiague, NY. It had parking for 2,500 cars and indoor seating for 1,200; a full service restaurant; a kid's playground; and a shuttle train to carry customers from their cars to the amenities. It was all contained on a 28-acre piece of land. The smallest drive-in theater is shared by two facilities the Harmony Drive-In, Harmony, PA and the Highway Drive-In, Bamburg, SC.

The Drive-In Church

Organized religion has never been slow in picking up a good idea. However, it may be the Anglicans that get credit for the first Drive-In Church. In September of 1950, the Canadian Churchman, an Anglican Church magazine, reported that there were 60 cars in attendance at the first drive-in service in Winnipeg. The service was conducted by Canon R. J. Pierce, Warden on St. John's College.

In the U.S., it was Florida that took the lead in motorized religion. The Daytona Beach Drive-In Christian Church (Disciples of Christ) opened it's Sunday morning service in 1953 in the former Neptune Drive-In Theater. Rev. Larry Deitch delivers his morning sermon today from a pulpit just below where the projection screen once stood. Communion is celebrated weekly. So, to accommodate the congregation sitting in their cars, a communion kit is given to parishioners as they enter the church grounds along with their bulletins. It wouldn't be a church without an offering. Golf carts facilitate the contribution process in Daytona Beach Drive-In Church. Eighty people attended the first service in 1953, the church attracts over 700 people weekly. Up until 1960 the church and theater co-existed. Deitch has heard his share of complaints from Christians who consider his church unorthodox. His answer is "I did church indoors for 30 years. Then I decided to go and do it like Jesus, outdoors by the seashore."

The drive-in concept went west two years later. It was 1955 when Rev. Robert Schuller conducted his first service from the top of the snack bar at the Orange Drive-In Theater in Orange, CA. Schuller's slogan in those early days was "Come as you are in your family car." Currently, his ministry and congregation is housed in the Crystal Cathedral (another roadside attraction) in Garden Grove, CA and still provides for people to attend in their cars.

EPILOGUE

Games to Pass Away the Time

As an only child, the worst thing about a road trip when I was young was the sheer boredom a car trip represented. Happy road trips included a family member or friend, near my own age, and the games that passed the time between stops. Interstate highways, back seat mounted DVD and VHS player televisions and a ever increasing number of battery powered electronic games have all but replaced the road trip games. But, I still remember a few that we played.

Counting Cows

I realized, when trying to explain this game in print, how absolutely insane it really is but I spent many hours as an ardent player.

Players split up on either side of the back seat, each responsible for his/her side. The object is to count the numbers of cows, worth one point each, that the player passes. (See, that's

why Interstate travel diminished interest in this game). A white horse was worth 10 points. Pass a school and all of your cows go inside for an education. Pass a cemetery your cows all die. Either way you go back to zero. Players agree on the number of cows that win.

Alphabet Signs

This, too, takes two players, one on either side of the car. Starting with the letter "A", players must alternate through the alphabet finding letters on signs along the side of the road. Playing this game in the South is easier because finding a "Q" is usually the most difficult letter. Why in the South? Barbeque.

An alternative way to play this game is to use license plates to find the letters.

I Spy

The game is to say a sentence that starts with "I Spy" and describe something you see without saying what it is. For instance, I spy something that is red and has four wheels. Say you are able to see a red Volkswagen but it could be other things like a fire chief's car. You get the idea.

Recently our young granddaughter was traveling with her mother, sister and maternal grandmother. A game of "I Spy" started. The little one stated, loudly, "I spy something that is old and drinks too much wine." A moment of silence followed then roars of laughter. Moments before the mother and grandmother were discussing needing to buy some wine.

"I Spy" is enjoying a renaissance of some degree thanks to the efforts of the Moose in the animated feature Brother Bear. "I spy something green, ay." "Tree." "I spy something tall." "Tree," and so on.

"I spy the last page of this book."

ABOUT THE AUTHOR

Ralph E. Jarrells retired from a successful career in marketing, advertising and publishing that included senior executive positions with major corporations, including Sr. VP Marketing with an international franchise company, VP Marketing with a NYSE company, VP Account Supervisor for the world's largest advertising company, and Editorial director for a major trade magazine publishing company.

He left corporate America to create his own award winning video production company, specializing in video programming for ministry and mission organizations. His work has since received 18 international creative awards.

In addition to *The Essential Automobile*, Jarrells is also the author of the supernatural thriller, ***Ill Gotten Gain***, a plausible yet fictional account of the movement in time and space of the 33 coins Judas was given for betraying Christ.

Also Available From

WORDCRAFTS PRESS

Confounding the Wise
by Dan Kulp

Letters at Midnight
by Roland B. King

What the Dog Said
by Joanne Brokaw

Past the Hood Ornament
by Mike Carmichael

Scrambled Hormones
by Monica Cane

www.wordcrafts.net

www.ingramcontent.com/pod-product-compliance
Lightning Source LLC
Chambersburg PA
CBHW051248020426
42333CB00025B/3113